D1524783

SERIES TITLES

PREHISTORY	I	XIII	SETTLING THE AMERICAS	
MESOPOTAMIA AND THE BIBLE LANDS	II	XIV	ASIAN AND AFRICAN EMPIRES	
ANCIENT EGYPT AND GREECE	III	XV	THE INDUSTRIAL REVOLUTION	
THE ROMAN WORLD	IV	XVI	ENLIGHTENMENT AND REVOLUTION	
ASIAN CIVILIZATIONS	V	XVII	NATIONALISM AND THE ROMANTIC MOVEMENT	
AMERICAS AND THE PACIFIC	VI	XVIII	THE AGE OF EMPIRE	
EARLY MEDIEVAL TIMES	VII	XIX	NORTH AMERICA: EXPANSION, CIVIL WAR, AND EMERGENCE	
BEYOND EUROPE	VIII	XX	TURN OF THE CENTURY AND THE GREAT WAR	
LATE MEDIEVAL EUROPE	IX	XXI	VERSAILLES TO WORLD WAR II	
RENAISSANCE EUROPE	X	XXII	1945 TO THE COLD WAR	
VOYAGES OF DISCOVERY	XI	XXIII	1991 TO THE 21ST CENTURY	
BIRTH OF MODERN NATIONS	XII	XXIV	ISSUES TODAY	

This Zak Books edition was published in 2009.
Zak Books is an imprint of McRae Books Srl.

ENLIGHTENMENT AND REVOLUTION
was created and produced by McRae Books Srl
Via del Salviatino, 1 – 50016 – Florence (Italy)
info@mcraebooks.com
www.mcraebooks.com

Publishers: Anne McRae, Marco Nardi
Series Editor: Anne McRae
Author: Neil Morris
Main Illustrations: Giorgio Albertini pp. 44–45;
Giacinto Gaudenzi pp. 18–19, 20–21, 24–25, 32–33;
Inklink p. 42; MMcomunicazione (M. Cappon, M.
Favilli, C. Scutti) pp. 12–13, 32–33; Andrea Ricciardi
di Gaudesi pp. 34–35; Sergio 40–41

Other Illustrations: Andrea Ricciardi di Gaudesi,
Studio Stalio (Alessandro Cantucci, Fabiano
Fabbrucci, Margherita Salvadori)
Maps: Paola Baldanzi
Photography: Bridgeman Art Library, London: pp. 7b,
8–9b, 10b, 17b, 23t, 27b, 29t, 37b, 39t
Scala Archives, Florence p. 15
Art Director: Marco Nardi
Layouts: Starry Dog Books Ltd
Project Editor: Loredana Agosta
Research: Loredana Agosta
Repro: Litocolor, Florence

Consultant: Dr. Joseph Bergin is Professor of Modern
History at Manchester University and Fellow of the
British Academy. His research interests are mainly in
the religious, social and political history of early
modern France from the later sixteenth to the
eighteenth century.

Library of Congress Cataloging-in-Publication Data

Enlightenment and Revolution
 ISBN 9788860981783

2009923557

Printed and bound in Malaysia.

Enlightenment and Revolution

Neil Morris

Consultant: Dr. Joseph Bergin, Professor of Modern History at Manchester
University and Fellow of the British Academy.

Zak
BOOKS

Contents

5 Introduction

6 The Eighteenth Century

8 The Enlightenment

10 France on the Eve of Revolution

12 Spain and Portugal

14 Italy

16 The Holy Roman Empire

18 The Rise of Prussia

20 Russia Comes to Power

22 Catherine the Great

24 The Turkish Wars

26 Poland and Scandinavia

28 The Grand Tour

30 The Low Countries

32 Great Britain

34 Eighteenth-Century Society

36 The Scientific Revolution

38 Eighteenth-Century Arts and Architecture

40 Eighteenth-Century Music

42 The French Revolution

44 Revolutionary Wars

46 Glossary

47 Index

Frederick the Great was an "enlightened despot" and one of the greatest rulers in European history.

TIMELINE

	1700	1720	1730	1740
FRANCE 		Louis XV becomes king at the age of five.		
SPAIN AND PORTUGAL	Death of King Charles II of Spain, the last of the Spanish Habsburgs. Philip V becomes king.	Philip V abdicates in favor of his son Luis, but returns when Luis dies.		Reign of Ferdinand VI of Spain.
ITALY	Austrian troops enter Naples.	Victor Amadeus II of Savoy exchanges Sicily for Sardinia. Vivaldi composes *The Four Seasons*.		Milan is ceded to the Habsburgs.
THE HOLY ROMAN EMPIRE AND PRUSSIA 	Reign of Joseph I as ruler of Austria and Holy Roman Emperor. Reign of Frederick William I as King of Prussia.			Maria Theresa rules as Archduchess of Austria and Queen of Hungary and Bohemia. Reign of Frederick II ("the Great") of Prussia.
RUSSIA AND EASTERN EUROPE 	Reign of Peter I ("the Great") of Russia. Reign of Ottoman sultan Ahmed III.	Persia cedes western and southern shores of the Caspian Sea to Russia in return for military aid. Reign of Ottoman Sultan Mahmud I.		Reign of Elizabeth of Russia.
POLAND AND SCANDINAVIA 	The Great Northern War is fought against Sweden by Russia, Denmark-Norway, and Saxony-Poland.		War of the Polish Succession, in which France, Spain, and Sardinia oppose Russia and Austria. Reign of Augustus III in Poland.	
LOW COUNTRIES 	William III, Prince of Orange, is stadholder of the Netherlands (and king of Great Britain).			William IV of Orange and Nassau becomes stadholder of the United Provinces.
GREAT BRITAIN 	England, Wales, and Scotland pass the Act of Union, forming Great Britain.		Sir Robert Walpole becomes the British prime minister.	In the Battle of Culloden Charles Edward Stuart's Scottish highlanders are crushed by the English.

Introduction

Madame de Pompadour (1721–64) was the mistress of Louis XV of France. She had great influence on French policies and was a patron of the arts.

The 18th century in Europe was an age of enlightenment and revolution. The movement known as the Enlightenment, which took place during the so-called Age of Reason, developed from the beliefs and theories of great French thinkers and writers. They furthered scientific advances and advocated a liberal approach to social reform. Some of Europe's monarchs adopted many of the proposed reforms in theory, but internal struggles and international conflicts made them difficult to carry through. Unfortunately these great ideas had little effect on the lives of ordinary people, and dissatisfaction caused by the growing class conflict laid the foundations for revolution.This book covers the major nations, empires, monarchs, and wars, and details developments in science, art, architecture, and music. By the end of the 18th century, the French Revolution had changed a nation and was making its impact felt throughout the continent and the world.

Louis XVI was executed by guillotine in Paris in 1793. His severed head was held up to the huge crowd.

1750	1760	1770	1780	1790
Denis Diderot's *Encyclopédie* is published.		The reign of Louis XVI begins.	The National Assembly approves the Declaration of the Rights of Man.	Storming of the Bastile, the French Revolution begins. Louis XVI is executed. The Reign of Terror begins.
Reign of Joseph I in Portugal, during which period the Marquess de Pombal is chief minister.	Reign of Charles III of Spain.		Reign of Maria I and consort Peter III (to 1786) in Portugal.	
		Reign in Tuscany of Grand Duke Peter Leopold, who transforms administration and law.		The last ruler of Venice is deposed, and the city falls to Austria.
The Seven Years' War, in which Maria Theresa is forced by Prussia to give up claims to Silesia. The composer Mozart is born.	Reign of Joseph II as Holy Roman Emperor.		Reign of Frederick William II of Prussia.	Reign of Leopold II as Holy Roman Emperor and king of Hungary and Moravia. Reign of Francis II as the last Holy Roman Emperor.
Tensions and rising taxes lead to a revolt in Sarajevo (in Bosnia-Herzegovina) against the Ottoman sultan.	Reign of Catherine II, "the Great" of Russia. First Russo–Turkish War.	Reign of Ottoman Sultan Abdulhamid.	Russian annexation of the Crimea from the Turks. Second Russo–Turkish War.	Reign of Paul I of Russia.
	Reign of Christian VII over Denmark and Norway.	First partition of Poland between Russia, Prussia, and Austria.		Second and third partitions of Poland. Denmark frees its serfs.
			Patriot Revolution. Prussian troops occupy Amsterdam.	Period of the Batavian Republic The Dutch East India Company is dissolved.
The Seven Years' War leads to Britain winning control of France's North American empire.	Reign of George III.			

The Eighteenth Century

The institution of absolute monarchy was threatened in many countries during the 18th century. The new philosophy of the Enlightenment spread from France, where before the end of the century social revolution toppled the king and created a republic. Nationalism continued as a powerful force everywhere, however, fuelling wars between European nations. In Britain, the Industrial Revolution was getting underway, and scientific advances were made across the continent.

Feeding the poor in the early 18th century. In 1709 a long period of freezing weather caused food shortages in Paris.

Right: Portrait of Isabella Godin, who traveled to the Amazon region as the wife of a scientific explorer.

Scientific Studies

At the beginning of the century Isaac Newton (1642–1727), widely considered one of the greatest scientists of all time, and others were making great discoveries in astronomy, mathematics, and other subjects (see pages 36–37). Their work built on and furthered the scientific revolution that had begun in the 16th century. The great thinkers of the Enlightenment period believed that an understanding of scientific processes was essential for all educated people.

Growing Unrest

Living conditions did not improve for most of Europe's poor people. Many farming families moved to the growing towns, where work and decent accommodation were not always available. At the same time successful business people of the new middle class were beginning to enjoy a wealthy lifestyle. Poverty and class conflict caused growing unrest among the working classes, leading to social revolution toward the end of the century.

A New Philosophy

Leading 18th-century thinkers presented a view of the world based on reason, scientific enquiry, and individualism, rather than on traditional values. This movement came to be known as the Enlightenment, and the period as the Age of Reason (see pages 8–9). Important rational thinkers believed that their approach enlightened others, bringing them greater knowledge and understanding about the world around them.

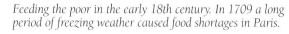

Left: Decorated title of the Declaration of the Rights of Man of 1789 (see pages 42–43).

This longcase clock was made in France about 1755. By mid-century, inventors had developed most of the devices found in modern mechanical clocks.

Great thinkers of the age gathered in the fashionable salons of Paris, where they discussed issues of the day.

MAJOR WARS

1701–14
War of the Spanish Succession (see page 12).

1733–38
War of the Polish Succession (see page 26).

1740–48
War of the Austrian Succession (see page 16).

1756–63
Seven Years' War (Britain and Prussia against Austria, France, and Russia).

1778–79
War of the Bavarian Succession (between Austria and Prussia, in which no battles were fought).

1792–1802
French Revolutionary Wars (see pages 44–45).

On the Battlefield

Four European wars of the 18th century were caused by disputes over who should succeed to the throne. They are the Wars of the Spanish, Polish, Austrian, and Bavarian Successions (for dates, see above). These and other wars had profound social effects, as monarchs and governments did everything they could to raise funds to support armies and finance campaigns.

Right: Painting by John Wootton of the Battle of Blenheim, fought in Bavaria in 1704. This was an important battle in the War of the Spanish Succession.

London financiers organize the Bank of England, which was set up at the end of the 17th century to raise money to finance war against France.

Right to the Throne

Ideas of monarchy changed dramatically in many parts of Europe. The changes were most pronounced in France. In 1700 Louis XIV was conducting his reign of splendor. By 1795 Louis XVI had been executed, the French monarchy had ended, and Napoleon Bonaparte was putting down a rebellion against the republican government. Before then, many so-called "enlightened despots" (see page 8) had introduced social and political reforms.

Frederick the Great extended Charlottenburg Palace in Berlin in the 1740s.

The Enlightenment

The Enlightenment, or Age of Reason, was an 18th-century philosophical and intellectual movement in Europe. Leading philosophers and writers, especially in France, put forward a view of the world that was based on reason and scientific enquiry. They believed that this approach helped people to help themselves, by improving their individual lives as well as society as a whole. This rational approach brought about important advances in the sciences and mathematics, and influenced European leaders in their approach to their subjects.

Knowledge, Freedom, and Happiness: Rational Goals

The enlightened thinkers of the Age of Reason believed the main goals of rational human beings to be knowledge, freedom, and happiness. They celebrated the power of reason, which allows all men and women to understand the universe and improve their own condition. The French philosopher and jurist Montesquieu put forward the belief that an understanding of rational laws could lessen the problems of society and improve people's lives.

Right: Denis Diderot (1713–84), and a page from the Encyclopédie *on the art of writing. Both Rousseau and Voltaire wrote articles for the* Encyclopédie.

Sculpture by Claude Michel of Baron de Montesquieu (1689–1755), whose major work was The Spirit of the Laws.

Religion and Deism

The philosophers of the Enlightenment accepted the existence of a creator God on the basis of reason. They believed that this supreme being created the universe and its physical laws, but then did not intervene in it. This rationalistic approach to religion and creation–known as deism–went against conventional religious faith, including Christianity. Some deists developed openly critical views of the Christian church and its practices.

The Powers of Reason

The group of French philosophers and writers known as the *philosophes*, which included Diderot, Rousseau, and Voltaire, believed in the ultimate power of reason. They held that the application of human reason showed the way to truth. Diderot was the chief editor of the 28-volume *Encyclopédie* (1751–72), to which more than 200 scholarly experts contributed. This monumental work presented a rational approach to the sciences, arts, and professions.

This crown coin of 1787 shows Joseph II, Holy Roman Emperor from 1765 to 1790. He introduced reforms in education and law.

Enlightened Despots

Enlightenment ideas captured the attention of several European rulers and influenced their approach to power. These so-called "enlightened despots" included Catherine the Great of Russia (see pages 22–23), Frederick the Great of Prussia (see pages 18–19), and Joseph II of Austria (see page 17). They remained authoritarian rulers (or despots), but used their power to introduce enlightened reforms.

The Swiss philosopher Jean-Jacques Rousseau (1712–78) influenced deist ideas. His novel Émile *offended the ecclesiastical authorities.*

The Salons

In the salons of Paris, well-connected women hosted fashionable gatherings that fostered philosophical and political debate. The *philosophes* were welcome guests, and these events helped them bring their ideas to the attention of influential men and women in French society. The Marquise de Pompadour, mistress of Louis XV, was helpful in resisting efforts to censor the *Encyclopédie*.

Left: At the Parisian salon of Marie-Thérèse Geoffrin, an actor reads a Voltaire play beneath a bust of the author. Encyclopaedists Jean d'Alembert and Denis Diderot are among those present.

France on the Eve of Revolution

The three kings of 18th-century France—Louis XIV, XV, and XVI—were faced with a society being fed revolutionary ideas about government and power by the country's enlightened thinkers. Reforms were needed, but they were generally opposed by the country's clergy and aristocracy. Life for the peasants and workers who paid most taxes became even harder as France's financial crisis deepened. There were food shortages, and the starving people protested by turning against their rulers. Revolution was in the air.

The bejewelled crown of Louis XV, which he wore at his coronation in 1722.

The *Ancien Régime*

The ideas of 18th-century French philosophers challenged the notion of absolute monarchy. Many people no longer believed that a king or queen ruled by divine right, and they looked forward to a new order. Late in the century they began to refer to the political and social system that they wished to replace as the *ancien régime*, or "old order." This was clearly a term of disapproval.

This painting by Louis de Boulogne of the young king exercising power is entitled Louis XV Granting Patents of Nobility to the Municipal Body of Paris.

King Louis XV

The great-grandson of Louis XIV (ruled 1643–1715), the young Louis XV succeeded him on his death but was not crowned until seven years later. For some years France was governed by a regent. In 1743 Louis took over rule without a chief minister, but he was weak and indecisive. He was seen as living in luxury while the people endured great hardship. Colonial losses in the Seven Years' War increased the king's unpopularity.

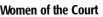

The Three Estates

French society was made up of three estates (or orders): The First Estate was made up of the clergy and the Second Estate of the nobility. The Third Estate comprised everyone else, including prosperous middle-class merchants, lawyers, officials, and–the largest group–peasants and workers. Most of the country's taxes came from the Third Estate, which caused great resentment, especially when they saw them wasted on foreign wars and court extravagance.

Above: People had to queue for rationed bread. Failed harvests caused rising prices and food shortages for the Third Estate.

Right: This cartoon illustrates the burdens of the Third Estate. A peasant literally carries the weight of a clergyman and a noble.

ANCIEN REGIME

1715–74
Reign of Louis XV, who becomes king at the age of five; the Duke of Orleans acts as regent until 1723.

1726
Louis's former tutor Cardinal de Fleury becomes head of government.

1733–38
War of the Polish Succession, in which France is allied to Spain.

1740–48
War of the Austrian Succession, in which France is allied to Prussia.

1756–63
The Seven Years' War, which ends with the loss to Britain of French colonies in Canada and India.

1770
Dauphin Louis, grandson of Louis XV, marries Marie Antoinette of Austria.

1774–92
Reign of Louis XVI.

1789
The king is forced to call an assembly of the States General (the first since 1614).

Women of the Court

Louis XV was married to Maria Leszczynska, daughter of the exiled king of Poland. In 1745, he gave one of his young favorites the title Marquise de Pompadour and made her his official mistress. The king was influenced by her political advice, which included involvement in the Seven Years' War. There were other favorites, including the Comtesse du Barry, who took over as royal mistress in 1769. This situation caused constant jealousy and scheming at court.

Portrait of Louis XVI in his royal robes.

Failed Reforms

Louis XVI appointed Robert Turgot to run the country's finances, but his attempts to reduce the public debt were opposed by both clergy and nobility. Louis replaced him with banker Jacques Necker, but his proposed reforms also met opposition from Marie Antoinette and the aristocracy. Wars increased the national debt, and the king was forced to call an assembly of the States General, representing the three estates. The following month, the Third Estate declared itself a National Assembly.

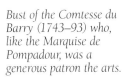

Bust of the Comtesse du Barry (1743–93) who, like the Marquise de Pompadour, was a generous patron the arts.

SPAIN AND PORTUGAL

1700
Death of King Charles II of Spain, the last of the Spanish Habsburgs.

1700–24 and 1724–46
Reign of Philip V of Spain.

1703
The Methuen Treaty seals an alliance and trade agreement between Portugal and England.

1724
Philip V abdicates in favor of his son Luis, but returns when Luis dies.

1746–59
Reign of Ferdinand VI of Spain.

1750–77
Reign of Joseph in Portugal, with Marquess de Pombal as chief minister.

1759–88
Reign of Charles III of Spain.

1763
Spain loses Florida to Britain; regains it in 1783.

1777–1816
Reign of Maria I and consort Peter III (to 1786) in Portugal.

1787
Charles III sets up a council of state to coordinate national policy.

The War of Spanish Succession

Charles II's lack of an heir led to the Spanish crown being taken by the Bourbon Duke of Anjou (grandson of Louis XIV) as Philip V. This led to the War of the Spanish Succession (1701–14), when a grand alliance of England, the Dutch Republic, and the Holy Roman Emperor declared war on Spain and France. Philip was finally recognized as king in 1713, but he lost many territories to Austria and Britain under the Treaty of Utrecht. He turned to creating a centralized administration in Spain.

Philip V is portrayed here conquering heresy in the form of a dragon.

Spain and Portugal

The Bourbon rule of Spain led to many disastrous battles, but it also helped bring Aragon, Catalonia, and Valencia under royal control. During the 18th century the Bourbon rulers introduced many reforms, such as lower taxes. There were strong family ties with the French, and great conflict with Britain, over Gibraltar, Minorca, and power in the Americas. Portugal had been ruled by the Braganza Dynasty since 1640, but the most important administrator of enlightened reforms was a government minister, the Marquess de Pombal.

Spain's Enlightened Despot

Philip V's son and successor, Charles III, was one of Europe's "enlightened despots" (see page 8). He introduced many of the changes that came to be known as the Bourbon Reforms. He and his advisers developed the Spanish economy, encouraging manufacture and freeing up trade. Resenting the power of the Jesuits, Charles expelled them from Spain and its colonies in 1767.

Right: Detail by Goya of the Count of Floribanda (1728–1808), a minister of Charles III who pushed through his reforms.

SPANISH BOURBON TERRITORIES 1789

Map labels:
- LA CORUÑA
- PARMA
- SPAIN
- VALENCIA
- NAPLES
- MEDITERRANEAN SEA
- PALERMO
- KINGDOM OF NAPLES
- ORUNO

Recovered Possessions

The War of the Polish Succession (1733–38) led to Spain gaining the Kingdom of Naples and Sicily, which was ruled by the future Spanish king Charles III. Under the peace treaty, Parma and Piacenza were given to Austria. But both territories, along with Guastalla, were restored to Spain by the terms of the Treaty of Aix-la-Chapelle at the end of the War of the Austrian Succession in 1748. The map shows the European territories of Bourbon Spain in 1789.

Spanish Bourbon Territories, 1789

Huge waves followed a terrible earthquake on 1 November 1755, overwhelming ships in Lisbon harbor. Flooding and fires destroyed much of the city and killed about 60,000 people.

Portugal

By formal agreement there was steady trade between Portugal and England during the 18th century, which helped both countries. Portugal succeeded in retaining its independence from Spain under the rule of John V (1706–50) and his successor Joseph. Real power was in the hands of the Marquess de Pombal, who as a believer in enlightened despotism reformed Portuguese administration and modernized education. Pombal also organized the rebuilding of Lisbon after the earthquake of 1755.

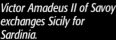

ITALY

1707
Austrian troops enter Naples.

1720
Victor Amadeus II of Savoy exchanges Sicily for Sardinia.

1727–31
Antonio Farnese rules the duchy of Parma and Piacenza.

1748
Milan is ceded to the Habsburgs.

1759–67
Bernardo Tanucci leads a council of regency to rule Naples-Sicily until Ferdinand IV (son of Charles VII) comes of age.

1765
Administrative reorganization in Milan with creation of a Supreme Economic Council.

1765–90
Reign in Tuscany of Grand Duke Peter Leopold, who transforms administration and law.

1768
The republic of Genoa hands its last overseas possession, Corsica, to France.

1797
The last doge (or ruler) of Venice is deposed, and the city falls to Austria.

1799
Lucca falls to the French.

Rome's Trevi Fountain was commissioned by Pope Clement XII in 1732. Designed by Nicolo Salvi, it was completed in 1762.

The Papal States
The Papal States had lost political and economic strength during the 17th century, and this trend continued. Successive popes tried to centralize power, but they failed to improve the poor economic situation. Corruption and bribery were rife, and the papacy's influence declined within the region and throughout Europe. Rome itself had brilliant squares, palaces, and official buildings, but much of the city was still poorly paved and had little sanitation.

Right: This Venetian coin of 1789 bears the name of the last doge, Ludovico Manin.

Italy

Many of the Italian states were greatly affected by events following the Wars of the Spanish Succession and Polish Succession (see pages 12–13). Peace settlements and treaties resulted in most falling into Spanish and Austrian hands. Some of the less powerful states did manage to retain their independence. Despite its declining political influence, including that of the Papal States, the Italian region remained an important focal point for the arts and sciences.

The House of Savoy
The House of Savoy (originally from the western Alps region) had acquired Piedmont in the 14th century. By the Treaty of Utrecht in 1713, Victor Amadeus II's status was raised from duke to king, as ruler of Sicily. In 1720 the Savoyard king was forced by the Austrian Habsburgs to exchange Sicily for Sardinia (then a Spanish possession). He and his successors ruled from their capital of Turin, in Piedmont, and their kingdom is often called Piedmont-Sardinia.

Left: The Basilica of Superga, on a hill to the east of Turin, was commissioned by Victor Amadeus II. It was designed by the Sicilian architect Filippo Juvarra in 1717 and completed in 1731.

Detail from a Goya painting of Charles III in hunting pose.

ITALY IN THE 18TH CENTURY

Spanish and Austrian Control of Italian Lands

Much of the Italian peninsula came under the control of the Spanish and Austrian Habsburgs. The map shows these lands, as well as the Papal States and other independent states. Some regions changed hands several times. The duchy of Parma and Piacenza, for example, was held by the Farnese family until 1731, when it passed to Don Carlos (the future Charles III of Spain). Two years later it came under Austrian control, but was returned to the Spanish Bourbons in 1748.

SAVOY · MILAN · PARMA · VENICE · GENOA · FLORENCE · TUSCANY · ADRIATIC SEA · ROME · NAPLES · SARDINIA · MEDITERRANEAN SEA · PALERMO · SICILY

Hapsburg Territory, 1715
To Hapsburgs, 1737
Savoy, 1715
To Savoy, 1720
To Spain, 1748
To Spain 1735

Tuscany

In 1737, on the death of Gian Gastone de' Medici, the title of Grand Duke of Tuscany passed to Francis Stephen, Duke of Lorraine (husband of Maria Theresa, later Holy Roman Emperor Francis I). This began the rule of the Habsburg-Lorraine family. Under Francis and his son Grand Duke Leopold I (later Holy Roman Emperor Leopold II), there was a period of reform. The church's privileges were reduced and internal trade barriers were lifted.

Independent States

Some of the northern states remained independent. The republics of Venice and Genoa were no longer the great powers that they had once been, but they did not embrace reform. The nobility continued to govern Venice, while Genoese trade had sunk to its lowest level by 1750. The commune of Lucca, in the northwest of Tuscany, had conflicts with powerful neighbors, but succeeded in keeping its independence until 1799.

This detail from a painting shows Holy Roman Emperor Francis I with two of his daughters in 1756.

Below: This painting by Canaletto shows the return of the Venetian state galley, the bucintoro. On Ascension Day every year until 1789, the galley was rowed out into the Adriatic Sea in a ceremony to wed Venice to the sea.

The Holy Roman Empire

By the start of the 18th century the former power of the Holy Roman Empire was all but gone. Though the emperors were in theory elected, the imperial crown was in practice inherited within the Habsburg Dynasty of Austria. Problems arose over the inheritance of power by a woman, Maria Theresa, leading to yet another European war of succession. Throughout the period there was conflict between Austria and Prussia, although there was agreement toward the end of the century over the division of Poland and concerns about revolutionary France.

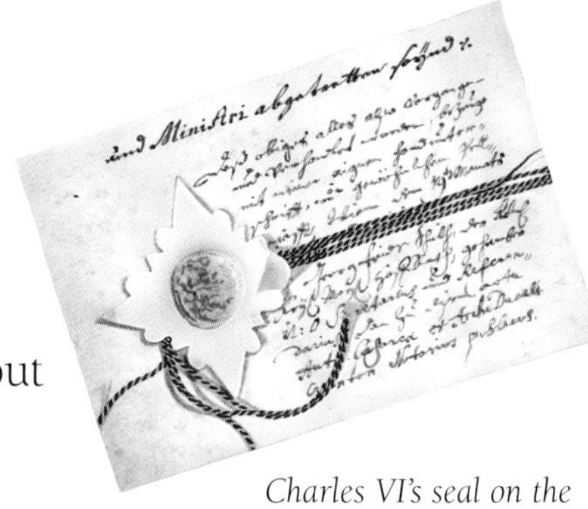

Charles VI's seal on the Pragmatic Sanction.

Charles VI's Pragmatic Sanction

Old laws prohibited a woman from inheriting kingdoms or empires. In 1713 Charles VI, having no son, drew up an imperial edict making his daughter Maria Theresa heir to all his Austrian territories. The emperor announced this publicly in 1724, and the major states agreed to recognize the edict. But on Charles' death in 1740, several broke their promise, leading to the War of the Austrian Succession.

HAPSBURG LANDS

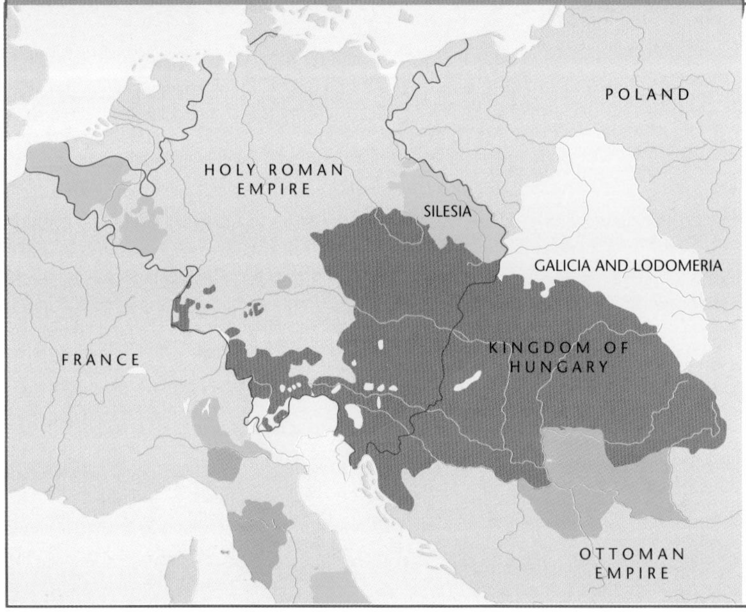

Marie Therese's Inheritance

The map shows the changes in Austrian Habsburg possessions during the 18th century. Having lost Silesia to Frederick II of Prussia in 1748, Maria Theresa strengthened her power in her own territory and built up a large army. She allied herself with France and Russia, but lost all claims to Silesia in the Seven Years' War. In 1772 she succeeded in gaining the territory of Galicia and Lodomeria during a partition of Poland.

- Austrian Hapsburg territory, 1700
- Silesia
- Peace of Utrecht 1713–1714
- 1718–1720
- 1737
- 1772–1805
- Border of Holy Roman Empire 1783

Francis I

Francis Stephen, the Duke of Lorraine, married Maria Theresa in 1736. When doing so, he agreed to give up Lorraine, but gained the duchy of Tuscany (see page 15). Nine years later, the duke became Holy Roman Emperor, but he was overshadowed by his powerful wife. He was not influential in government, leaving administration to the successful chancellor and foreign minister Kaunitz.

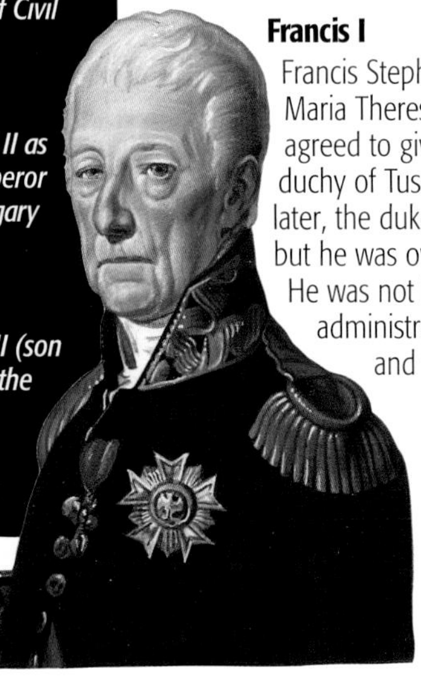

Count Wenzel Anton von Kaunitz, who was Austrian state chancellor from 1753 to 1792.

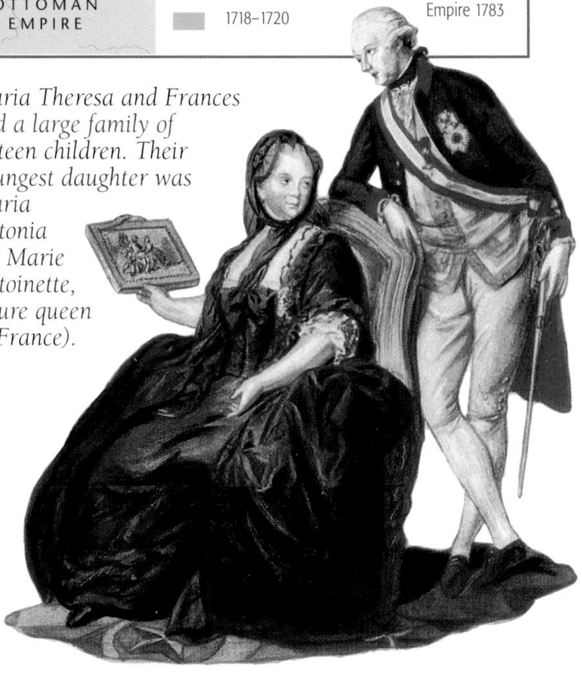

Maria Theresa and Frances had a large family of sixteen children. Their youngest daughter was Maria Antonia (or Marie Antoinette, future queen of France).

THE HOLY ROMAN EMPIRE

1705–11
Reign of Joseph I as ruler of Austria and Holy Roman Emperor during the War of the Spanish Succession (1701–14).

1711–40
Reign of Charles VI, brother of Joseph I, as ruler of Austria and Hungary (as Charles III) and Holy Roman Emperor.

1740–80
Maria Theresa rules as Archduchess of Austria and Queen of Hungary and Bohemia.

1745–65
Reign of Francis I, husband of Maria Theresa, as her co-regent and Holy Roman Emperor.

1748
The Treaty of Aix-la-Chapelle allows Maria Theresa to keep Austria, Bohemia, and Hungary.

1756–63
The Seven Years' War, in which Maria Theresa is forced by Prussia to give up claims to Silesia.

1765–90
Reign of Joseph II as Holy Roman Emperor.

1786
Joseph II issues a Universal Code of Civil Law.

1790–92
Reign of Leopold II as Holy Roman Emperor and King of Hungary and Moravia.

1792–1806
Reign of Francis II (son of Leopold II) as the last Holy Roman Emperor.

The Josephinum, in Vienna, was founded by Joseph II in 1785 as a medical academy. Today the building houses a Museum of Medical History.

Below: This painting shows Joseph II with his generals at a military camp.

Joseph II

From 1765 to 1780 Joseph II co-ruled with his mother, Maria Theresa. After her death, Joseph (one of Europe's "enlightened despots") tried to rationalize the imperial government. He reorganized the army, abolished serfdom, encouraged religious toleration and equality, and granted freedom of the press. Under his rule artistic life in Vienna flourished. His social reforms brought him into conflict with the clergy and nobility, but made him very popular with ordinary citizens.

Leopold II

Joseph II's younger brother Leopold was one of the most capable of the "enlightened despots." He succeeded his father Francis as Duke of Tuscany in 1765 and, after his brother's death in 1790, was elected emperor. Leopold upheld the reforms granting religious freedom to non-Catholics and emancipating the peasants, but in other areas he failed to carry through reforms. He was concerned by revolutionary events in France and concluded an alliance with Prussia before his death in 1792.

Above: The double-headed eagle was a symbol of power adopted by the Holy Roman Empire. All power was lost by the end of the 18th century.

PRUSSIA

1706
Frederick William I marries Sophia Dorothea, daughter of George Louis, elector of Hanover (later George I of England).

1713–40
Reign of Frederick William I as King of Prussia.

1719
End of serfdom in Prussia.

1720
Prussia gains Swedish Pomerania by the Treaty of Stockholm.

1740–86
Reign of Frederick II ("the Great").

1745–47
Frederick's rococo Sanssouci Palace is built at Potsdam to his own design.

1767
Publication of Minna von Barnhelm *by Gotthold Ephraim Lessing, German dramatist resident in Silesia who expresses Enlightenment ideals.*

1772
Formal recognition of Frederick's title as King of Prussia.

1781
Publication of Critique of Pure Reason *by philosopher Immanuel Kant, professor at Königsberg University, East Prussia.*

1786–97
Reign of Frederick William II, Frederick II's nephew.

The ancestral Hohenzollern Castle, in Swabia (southwest Germany), was built in the 15th century on the site of an earlier fortress.

The Hohenzollerns

The Hohenzollern family, originally from Swabia, rose to power in the state of Brandenburg. During the early 16th century they acquired the duchy of Prussia. In 1701 the Hohenzollern ruler Frederick III, elector of Brandenburg, assumed the title "king in Prussia" with the agreement of Holy Roman Emperor Leopold I. The Prussian kings kept their title of electors of Brandenburg until the end of the Holy Roman Empire.

Frederick William I

During his reign, Frederick William I (son of the founding Prussian king) created a more unified, efficient, and prosperous state. He streamlined the bureaucracy of government and ended corruption. Frederick William concentrated on military affairs and especially building up his army, introducing a form of conscription in 1733. He succeeded in leaving his son, Frederick II, a centralized state with solid finances and an excellent army.

The Rise of Prussia

Prussia became a powerful force in the 18th century. With a government based on authority and discipline, it had a famously strong, efficient army. Frederick the Great used his power both to expand the kingdom and to further the arts and sciences. He was one of Europe's most important "enlightened despots," believing in progress but ruling autocratically. By the end of his rule Prussia was a large, unified kingdom, stretching from the old border with Hanover in the west to the new, reduced Poland in the east.

The Prussian Army

Frederick William I (nicknamed the "sergeant king") expanded the Prussian army from 38,000 men to about 83,000. As well as introducing conscription, he recruited from all over Europe. His army was famed for its loyal officers and disciplined infantry. They were trained by Prince Leopold of Anhalt-Dessau, a fearsome field marshal who introduced the iron ramrod and modern bayonet. Frederick II carried on the military tradition with his cavalry, which became the strongest mounted force in Europe.

Right: A Prussian grenadier in Frederick II's army. The new-style helmet replaced a peaked cap and was more practical for a grenade-thrower.

Detail from a Prussian grenadier's cap.

PRUSSIA

Map labels:
BALTIC SEA
POMERELIA
WEST PRUSSIA
EAST PRUSSIA
BRANDENBURG
SOUTH PRUSSIA
SILESIA
HOLY ROMAN EMPIRE
HAPSBURG EMPIRE

Brandenburg and acquisitions by Frederick the Great

Acquisitions from Poland, 1793

Acquisitions from Poland, 1795

— Border of Holy Roman Empire

Frederick the Great's Prussia

Just seven months after coming to power, Frederick II attacked the Habsburg province of Silesia. The conquest was secured at the end of the Seven Years' War, in which Prussia held off Austria, France, and Russia. Frederick acquired much of Pomerelia as his share of the partition of Poland, making this West Prussia and linking Brandenburg with the original Prussia to unify the state. The map shows the conquests and expansion of the Hohenzollern Prussian state.

An Enlightened Court

Frederick II supported the progressive ideas of the Enlightenment. He was a great admirer of Voltaire, who called him "the philosopher king." Frederick improved the Prussian legal and educational systems, and encouraged religious tolerance. Promoting the arts, he surrounded himself with educated men and wrote on politics, history, and philosophy.

Above: Ivory flutes from Frederick's collection. The king was himself a skilled flautist.

Frederick the Great in discussion with his friend Voltaire in the gardens of Sanssouci Palace. The French philosopher visited the Prussian court in the 1750s.

Russia Comes to Power

As an important statesman and reformer, Peter the Great was responsible for bringing wider power to Russia in the early 1700s. His successors allowed more power to guards, nobles, and favorite advisers. The developing court culture was important to the autocratic rulers and aristocrats. There were many intrigues and coups at the highest level of society, but life did not generally improve for the growing empire's serfs.

In 1697 Peter the Great (in the striped tunic) disguised himself and worked as a ship's carpenter at the Dutch port of Zaandam. He later visited the British dockyard at Deptford.

The Navy

Peter I was always fascinated by ships and shipbuilding. He became a skilled shipwright, which enabled him to oversee the construction of the Russian navy. Hundreds of galleys joined with 52 battleships and many other craft to make up Peter's powerful fleet. This was used to annex part of the Baltic coast. The tsar had special schools set up to train young men for naval service.

Modernization

Peter the Great used his knowledge of Western technology and government to modernize Russia and make it a major European power. He created the first effective Russian regular army and expanded his territory to the Baltic Sea, gaining Ingria, Estonia, and Livonia. Having founded St. Petersburg, he made it his capital in 1712. Peter reformed Russian government and administration, as well as trade and industry, but dealt harshly with anyone who opposed him.

Above right: Practical and educational books flourished under Peter I. This page is from a children's book.

Catherine I

Peter's second wife, a Lithuanian woman of humble birth, joined the Russian Orthodox Church in 1703 and took the name Catherine. She married the tsar in 1712 and succeeded him through the power and support of guard regiments. Catherine gave control to a Supreme Privy Council made up of her late husband's advisers, who continued many of his policies.

This portrait is considered a flattering likeness of Empress Catherine I.

Above: A satirical woodcut of mice taking their tormentor, a large cat, to its burial. The cat represented Peter the Great, and the mice were those he persecuted.

Anna

After Peter II died on the day set for his wedding to a princess, the Supreme Privy Council offered the throne to Peter the Great's niece, Anna. The new empress promptly abolished the Council, but left affairs of state to a cabinet and German advisers. Anna treated opponents brutally and oversaw a reign of terror against peasants who could not pay their taxes.

Anna's gold and silver crown glittered with precious stones.

Detail of a painting of Elizabeth in 1743.

Elizabeth I

Elizabeth came to power in a coup, when guards arrested the infant emperor Ivan IV (then aged 15 months) and his mother and regent Anna Leopoldovna (niece of the late Empress Anna). The new empress left most matters to her trusted advisers, but she did encourage education and the arts. During her reign Russia stuck to a pro-Austrian foreign policy and fought successfully against Prussia in the Seven Years' War.

In 1754 Elizabeth commissioned her court architect Bartolomeo Rastrelli to rebuild the Winter Palace at St. Petersburg (right) in a baroque style. Rastrelli had completed the Summer Palace ten years earlier. Elizabeth's palaces were meant to compete with Versailles.

PETER THE GREAT'S SUCCESSORS

1696–1725
Sole reign of Peter I ("the Great") after his sister acted as regent (1682–89) and his half-brother as co-tsar (1689–96).

1700–21
The Great Northern War is fought against Sweden by Russia, Denmark-Norway, and Saxony-Poland.

1713
Russia loses Azov at the end of the Turkish War (1710–13).

1723
Persia cedes western and southern shores of the Caspian Sea to Russia in return for military aid.

1725–27
Reign of Catherine I, widow of Peter I.

1727–30
Reign of Peter II, grandson of Peter I, crowned at the age of 11.

1730–40
Reign of Anna, niece of Peter I.

1740–41
Regency during the reign of infant Ivan VI.

1741–62
Reign of Elizabeth, daughter of Peter I and Catherine I.

1752
The Catherine Palace is completed at Tsarskoe Selo by Rastrelli.

1755
Foundation of the University of Moscow.

Catherine The Great

Catherine the Great was very much influenced by the ideas of the Enlightenment, and she counts as one of the most important "enlightened despots." Having read widely among the major French philosophers of the age, including Montesquieu and Voltaire, she had many reforming ideas. Like Peter the Great before her, she expanded the Russian empire physically and gave it greater political significance in Europe during her 34-year reign.

Catherine Takes the Throne

In 1744 Princess Sophie of Anhalt-Zerbst, a small German principality, was received into the Russian Orthodox Church and took the name Yekaterina (Catherine). The following year she married Empress Elizabeth's nephew Peter, heir to the Russian throne. Six months after her weak husband succeeded Elizabeth as Peter III in 1762, guards officers overthrew the emperor with Catherine's approval. At the age of 33 she became Empress Catherine II, later known as "the Great." Eight days later her husband was murdered.

The rebel Pugachov was captured and taken in an iron cage to Moscow, where he was beheaded.

An English cartoon of Catherine being offered Warsaw and Constantinople by the devil.

Pugachev's Rebellion

In 1773 a former Cossack officer named Yemelyan Pugachov, claiming to be the dead emperor Peter III, started a peasant uprising. Pugachov's promise to free the serfs led to a rebellion that spread rapidly through the south-eastern provinces. The rebels killed at least 1,500 nobles and more than 1,000 government officials and were heading for Moscow before Catherine sent troops to crush them.

Copper kopeck of 1789, showing the imperial crown over Catherine's monogram.

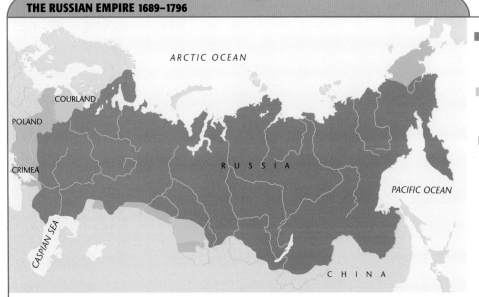

THE RUSSIAN EMPIRE 1689–1796

ARCTIC OCEAN

COURLAND

POLAND

CRIMEA

R U S S I A

PACIFIC OCEAN

CASPIAN SEA

C H I N A

Russia, 1689

Expansion under Peter the Great, 1689–1725

Expansion by the time of Catherine the Great's death, 1796

Territorial Expansion

Catherine continued the expansion of the empire that had begun with Peter the Great. The partitions of Poland gave Russia valuable territory in the west, and the third partition included annexation of the Baltic duchy of Courland. In the south, the taking of the Crimea from the Ottoman Turks gave the empire new territories along the Black Sea shore. The map shows Russian expansion during the reigns of Peter and Catherine.

Above: The neoclassical Green Dining Room, in the Catherine Palace at Tsarskoe Selo, was designed by the Scottish architect Charles Cameron in 1773.

Artistic Patronage

Catherine was an enthusiastic patron of the arts. She herself wrote satires, historical articles, and opera libretti, and corresponded with the French encyclopaedists (see page 8), including Diderot and Voltaire. She encouraged the translation of foreign works into Russian, and subsidized public performances of plays. The empress promoted the neoclassical style in architecture and decoration.

Above: The Tauride Palace in St. Petersburg was built in 1789 by the Russian architect Ivan Starov for Grigory Potemkin.

Portrait of Alexei Bobrinskoy painted in 1769

Catherine commissioned this colossal bronze statue of Peter the Great from French sculptor Étienne-Maurice Falconet. It was put up in St. Petersburg in 1782.

REIGN OF CATHERINE THE GREAT

1762
Six-month reign of Peter III, nephew of the late Empress Elizabeth.

1762–96
Reign of Catherine II, "the Great."

1767
Catherine prepares her Instruction, a document that recommends liberal government reform and a new legal code.

1772
First partition of Poland between Russia, Prussia, and Austria.

1775
Reorganization of Russia into provinces and districts.

1782
Catherine appoints a Commission on National Education that leads to the founding of many schools.

1783
Annexation of the Crimea from the Turks; an imperial opera and ballet theater is established in St. Petersburg, with the Kirov ballet company.

1787
Catherine makes a grand journey to the Crimea arranged by her former lover, Grigory Potemkin.

1793–95
Second and third partitions of Poland.

1796–1801
Reign of Paul, son of Catherine the Great.

Catherine's Children

Catherine's first child Paul, born in 1754, succeeded her as emperor. In 1757 Catherine gave birth to a daughter, Anna. Her third child, Alexei Bobrinskoy, was born during her husband's short reign in 1762.

THE TURKISH WARS

1703–30
Reign of Ottoman sultan Ahmed III (period also known as the Tulip Time).

1730–54
Reign of Sultan Mahmud I, who is advised by Comte de Bonneval, a French convert to Islam.

1739
Treaty of Belgrade, peace settlement between the Ottoman Turks and Russia (plus allied Austria).

1750
Tensions and rising taxes lead to a revolt in Sarajevo (in Bosnia-Herzegovina) against the Ottoman sultan.

1757–74
Reign of Sultan Mustafa III.

1768–74
First Russo–Turkish War.

1774–89
Reign of Sultan Abdulhamid.

1787–92
Second Russo–Turkish War.

1789–1807
Reign of Sultan Selim III, nephew of Abdulhamid.

The Treaty

The treaty of Kuchuk Kainarji, signed at Kaynardzha in present-day Bulgaria in 1774, ended the first Russo-Turkish War in favor of the Russians. It ceded several Black Sea ports to Russia, declared the Crimean khanate independent of the new Ottoman sultan Abdulhamid, and gave Russia the right to maintain a fleet on the Black Sea. The Russians were also allowed to represent and protect Greek Orthodox Christians in Ottoman territory.

The Balkan Peninsula

Peter the Great (see page 20) wanted to free the Balkans from Ottoman rule. In 1710 Sultan Ahmed III took his forces into the Northern War against Russia. When the campaign ended in victory for the Ottomans at the River Pruth the following year, the Russians were forced to return Azov to Turkey. War broke out again in 1735, with Russia and Austria allied against the Ottomans. The Russians gained little and agreed not to build a Black Sea fleet.

The Turks Declare War

Sultan Mustafa III declared war on Catherine the Great in 1768 after demanding that Russia stop interfering in the affairs of Poland. Two years later the Russian fleet won a great victory over the Ottomans at the harbor of Chesme on the Aegean Sea. This success inspired great confidence in the Russians among rebels within the Ottoman empire, making military success on land easier.

Above: Catherine the Great had the neo-Gothic Russian Orthodox Church of St. John built at Chesme Palace in St Petersburg in 1780. It commemorated the great naval victory.

Above: This cotton bolster cover embroidered with silk was made in the mid-18th century in the Epirus region of modern Greece. It was an important textile production center.

The Turkish Wars

During the 18th century Russia tried to continue its eastward expansion at the expense of the declining Ottoman Empire. The shores of the Black Sea, which formed an important access to world trade routes, were still in the hands of the Ottoman Turks and their vassals, the khans of Crimea. This situation and a wish by Russia to dominate the Balkan Peninsula, led to two major Russo-Turkish wars. Military victories and territorial gains led to increased Russian and European influence in Ottoman affairs.

Annexation of Crimea

Under the terms of the 1774 treaty, the territory of the Crimean khanate formed an independent state that was subject to the Ottoman sultan only in religious matters. Nine years later, Catherine annexed the Crimea outright. This led to many Crimean Tartars leaving their homeland, since they preferred to live under Ottoman rule. Their fertile lands were soon colonized by Russians.

Above: These ceremonial horse's knee guards were presented to Catherine the Great by Sultan Abdulhamid.

The Second Turkish War

War broke out again in 1787, with Holy Roman Emperor Joseph II on the side of the Russians. Joseph's army suffered terrible defeat, but Russian successes forced the Ottoman Turks to sign the Treaty of Jassy in 1792. This treaty gave the Russians a large stretch of Black Sea coast to the east of the Dniester River.

Painting of Sultan Selim III, who undertook a program of reform and Westernization within his empire.

Below: Catherine the Great arrives at the Khan's palace in Bakhchisarai, capital of the Crimean khanate, in 1787. She traveled there with a retinue of 2,300 people in order to take possession of her new province.

POLAND AND SCANDINAVIA

1697–1718
Reign of Charles XII in Sweden.

1700–21
The Great Northern War is fought against Sweden by Russia, Denmark-Norway, and Saxony-Poland.

1720–72
The so-called Age of Freedom in Sweden.

1733–38
War of the Polish Succession, in which France, Spain, and Sardinia oppose Russia and Austria.

1733–63
Reign of Augustus III in Poland.

1738–65
The Hats party is powerful in Sweden but lead the country to financial collapse.

1766
Future Gustav III of Sweden (reigned 1771–92) marries the daughter of Frederick V of Denmark (reigned 1746–66).

1766–1808
Reign of Christian VII over Denmark and Norway.

1780
Denmark agrees an armed neutrality treaty with Sweden and Holland and a special treaty with Britain.

Poland and Scandinavia

Important struggles and battles defined this region early in the 18th century. The Great Northern War, from which Russia emerged victorious, was quickly followed by the War of Polish Succession, in which Russia and Austria played a major part. Sweden was crushed in the Northern War, and later in the century its monarchy was reduced in power by an enlightened parliamentary government. By the end of the period Denmark was introducing reforms, while Poland was divided up by the major powers until it ceased to exist.

The Northern War

In 1697 Frederick Augustus, Elector of Saxony, was chosen from 18 candidates to be king of Poland. As Augustus II (later known as "the Strong"), he allied Saxony-Poland with Russia and Denmark and started the Great Northern War (1700–21) against Charles XII of Sweden by invading Livonia. Augustus was deposed in 1704 and restored by Russia six years later. By the end of the war, Russia was the major Baltic power.

SCANDINAVIA 1721

NORTH SEA

KINGDOM OF NORWAY AND DENMARK

SWEDEN

KARELIA

INGRIA

ESTONIA

LIVONIA

BALTIC SEA

- Sweden, 1721
- Kingdom of Norway and Denmark
- Swedish territory lost to Russia, 1721

The "Golden Rider," a gilded statue of Augustus the Strong, erected in Dresden in 1735.

The War of Polish Succession

After the death of Augustus the Strong, Polish nobles elected Stanislaw Leszczynski (father-in-law of Louis XV of France) as their king. But Russia and Austria forced Poland to accept Augustus's son, which led to war. France won territory from Austria, but a peace treaty confirmed Augustus III as king of Poland. Stanislaw was compensated by being made Duke of Lorraine.

After the Great Northern War, Frederik IV of Denmark had a summer palace built beside Lake Esrum. The baroque building was named Fredensborg ("Palace of Peace").

Portrait of Stanislaw II Poniatowski, who reigned from 1764 to 1795 as the last king of independent Poland.

Denmark and Norway

The Danish-controlled union between Denmark and Norway continued in the 18th century. It developed an important merchant navy as well as a military fleet. In the 1780s the stagnant Danish economy and society were revitalized by land reforms that included the abolition of serfdom. The reforms were a successful expression of "enlightened despotism."

Sweden
For Sweden the Great Northern War was disastrous, causing the loss of many territories. These included its Baltic provinces of Estonia, Livonia, Ingria, and Karelia. This map shows the situation in 1721. After the war, a new Swedish constitution gave great power to a legislative assembly that allowed parliamentary government, reducing the role of the monarchy.

This Sèvres vase was a gift from Gustav III of Sweden to Catherine II of Russia.

Allegorical illustration of the partition of Poland, showing Catherine the Great, Maria Theresa, Frederick II, and Joseph II dividing up the map.

Below: This painting of the election of Stanislaw II Poniatowski as Polish king in 1764 was completed 14 years later by the celebrated Venetian artist Bernardo Bellotto.

Growth of the Empire

Poland's weakness and disunity led to its being divided and finally completely absorbed by Austria, Prussia, and Russia in three separate partitions (1772, 1793, and 1795). The second partition led to a Polish uprising, but this was quickly put down. Russia received the most territory, but the capital, Warsaw, was taken by Prussia. Maria Theresa opposed the scheme, but Austria accepted its gains. The map shows how Poland was divided among the three invaders.

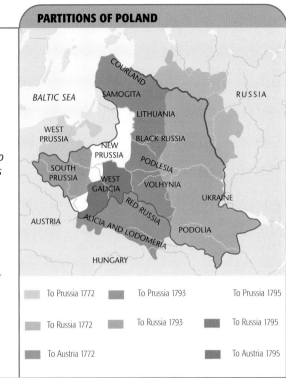

PARTITIONS OF POLAND

COURLAND
BALTIC SEA
SAMOGITA
RUSSIA
LITHUANIA
WEST PRUSSIA
NEW PRUSSIA
BLACK RUSSIA
SOUTH PRUSSIA
PODLESIA
WEST GALICIA
VOLHYNIA
RED RUSSIA
UKRAINE
AUSTRIA
GALICIA AND LODOMERIA
PODOLIA
HUNGARY

▢ To Prussia 1772	▨ To Prussia 1793	To Prussia 1795
▨ To Russia 1772	▨ To Russia 1793	▨ To Russia 1795
▨ To Austria 1772		▨ To Austria 1795

—— Boundary of Poland 1772

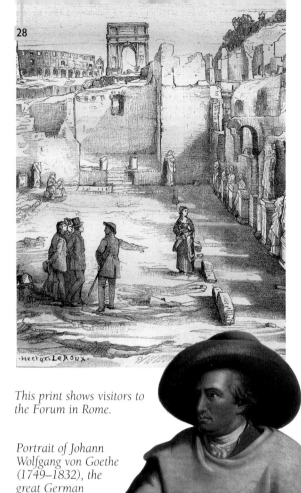

This print shows visitors to the Forum in Rome.

Portrait of Johann Wolfgang von Goethe (1749–1832), the great German writer, who traveled to Italy to study classical art. He later wrote his autobiographical Italian Journey.

The Grand Tour

It was fashionable during the 18th century for young upper-class Englishmen to undertake a cultural tour of Europe. This Grand Tour was seen as part of a young man's classical education, and he very often took his tutor and a servant with him. Noblemen and artists from other parts of Europe also traveled to pre-revolutionary France and Italy as part of their cultural development. The ultimate goal was Rome, and after 1750 some travelers even went on visit the remains of the ancient cities of Herculaneum and Pompeii.

Travel Accounts

The Grand Tour inspired many journals, travel accounts, and guidebooks. The first was *The Grand Tour, a Journey through the Netherlands, Germany, Italy, and France* by Thomas Nugent, published in 1749. One of the most famous journals was written by James Boswell, the Scottish biographer of Samuel Johnson. Boswell traveled through Europe to Italy in 1763–66. On his travels he met Jean-Jacques Rousseau, who encouraged him to visit Corsica. There he met the Corsican patriot Pasquale Paoli; Boswell wrote *An Account of Corsica*, which made him famous.

Right: Pompeo Batoni was famous for his portraits of tourists among the antiquities of Rome. This is a detail of his study of John Talbot, later 1st Earl Talbot, painted in 1783.

Paris

The culture and beauty of 18th-century Paris were well known. Visitors to the French capital were captivated by the sophistication of its high society. Many also took a trip to Versailles, the home of the French monarchy, where they could marvel at the magnificent palace and gardens. On their journeys many travelers took the opportunity to stay at the homes of their national envoys, who were not in a position to refuse hospitality.

Fashionable clothes were popular with visitors to Paris. This illustration from Diderot's Encyclopédie shows a tailor taking measurements.

Venice

The great attraction of Venice was as a center of pleasure. Many grand tourists made sure they visited the city at carnival time, during the week before Lent. They enjoyed gondola races and masked entertainments. Since the first public casino opened there in 1638, Venice had been known for its gaming houses. The tourist was offered full opportunity to spend (or lose) all his money.

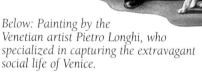

Below: Painting by the Venetian artist Pietro Longhi, who specialized in capturing the extravagant social life of Venice.

Rome

Arriving in Rome was the ultimate aim of many Grand Tourists. This was the center of historical antiquity and classical art. They visited all the famous ancient sites, including the Forum. James Boswell wrote of the Colosseum: "It is hard to tell whether the astonishing massiveness or the exquisite taste of this superb building should be more admired."

Florence

Florence was visited for its art treasures. On much of their journey, tourists had to gain entry to private collections in order to view classical and Renaissance paintings and sculptures. They were also keen to acquire works for their own collections at home. In Florence they could visit the Uffizi Gallery, as the German-born painter Johann Zoffany did in the 1770s. He was commissioned by George III of England to record the gallery's greatest masterpieces.

Above: This painting by Giovanni Paolo Pannini (1691–1765) shows the walls of the Gallery of Cardinal Silvio Valenti in Rome filled with works of art.

Detail of Zoffany's painting of English visitors admiring works in the Uffizi Gallery.

The Low Countries

THE LOW COUNTRIES

1672–1702
William III, Prince of Orange, is stadholder of the Netherlands (and king of Great Britain, 1689–1702).

1747
William IV, Prince of Orange and Nassau, is stadholder of all seven provinces of the United Netherlands.

1751–59
Anne of Hanover acts as regent for her son William V (stadholder 1751–95).

1767
William V marries Wilhelmina of Prussia, sister of the future King Frederick William II.

1780–84
Fourth Anglo-Dutch War

1781
Dutch nobleman and Patriot leader Joan van der Capellen tot den Pol (1741–84) issues an anonymous pamphlet To the People of the Netherlands, *advocating liberal democracy.*

1787
Prussian troops occupy Amsterdam and end the Patriot Revolution.

1795–1806
Period of the Batavian Republic.

1799
The Dutch East India Company is dissolved.

The region of the Low Countries covers the present-day territory of Belgium, Luxembourg, and the Netherlands. In the 18th century the region of the Dutch republic was governed for the most part by stadholders (chief magistrates or governors) of the House of Orange. During the century there were several revolts against this system of government, as more enlightened groups tried to reform the United Provinces. In 1795 the entire Low Countries fell to an invading French force.

Terracotta bust of William IV (1711–51) wearing the stadholder's ceremonial breastplate and cloak.

This porcelain cistern was designed for the Dutch East India Company by the Amsterdam artist Cornelis Pronk (1691–1759). It was manufactured in China around 1730 and then taken to Europe for sale.

United Provinces
After the death of William of Orange, there was no stadholder. The Dutch Republic was ruled by a group of hereditary noblemen acting as regents. When this system lost power in 1747 and French troops threatened to invade the republic, William IV, Prince of Orange and Nassau, became stadholder and united all seven provinces under his rule. The office of stadholder was also made hereditary in both male and female lines.

War with England
During the American War of Independence (1775–83) the United Provinces saw a trading opportunity for their merchants. They sided with and officially recognized the emerging United States of America. This led to war breaking out against Britain in 1780, but the Dutch navy had been neglected for many years and was overpowered by the British fleet. This disastrous defeat for the Dutch led to a rapid decline in their trading fortunes.

This silver 3-florin piece was issued in 1790, when the southern Netherlands was briefly independent.

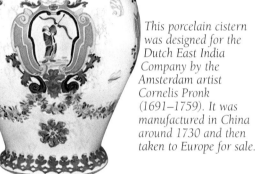

THE LOW COUNTRIES

NORTH SEA

UNITED PROVINCES

FRANCE

AUSTRIAN NETHERLANDS

Revolt Against Hapsburg Power
In 1713 the Spanish possessions in the Low Countries—covering the area of modern Belgium and Luxembourg—were transferred to the Austrian branch of the Hapsburgs. The map shows this territory, along with the seven Dutch provinces. In 1789 revolutionaries from Brabant led a revolt against the Holy Roman Emperor and defeated an Austrian force at Turnhout. Imperial authority was re-established in 1790 with little opposition.

　　United Provinces

　　Austrian Netherlands

───　Boundary of the Holy Roman Empire

The Patriotic Movement

Growing unrest led to the formation of a political movement that was influenced by the ideas and aims of French Enlightenment thinkers, as well as by French and American revolutionaries. The Dutch Patriots opposed the Orangists and stadholder government, and were determined that their policies should benefit the whole nation. In 1787 the Patriots were forced to flee to France.

The Last Stadholder

When William IV died in 1751, his young son succeeded him as stadholder. William V was a conservative and incompetent governor. After losing the war with Britain, the Patriots forced him to leave The Hague. The Prussians restored him, but after the French invasion of 1795 he was dismissed from office and fled to England and later to Nassau.

Wilhelmina of Prussia, wife of William V, was more strong-willed than her husband. She contributed to restoring the power of the position of stadholder.

Below: Patriots rioted in Amsterdam in 1784, attacking the homes of rich burghers.

Portrait of William V (1748–1806) by the German painter Johann Heinrich Wilhelm Tischbein.

GREAT BRITAIN

1702–14
Reign of Queen Anne (first British monarch from 1707).

1707
Parliaments of the Kingdom of England and Wales and the Kingdom of Scotland pass the Act of Union, forming Great Britain.

1714–27
Reign of George I, the first Hanoverian king.

1727–60
Reign of George II, son of George I.

1735
Sir Robert Walpole and his family move to 10 Downing Street, making it the residence of the British prime minister.

1746
Battle of Culloden, in which Charles Edward Stuart's Scottish highlanders are crushed by the English.

1751
English artist William Hogarth completes Beer Street *and* Gin Lane, *illustrations of London life.*

1756–63
The Seven Years' War leads to Britain winning control of France's North American empire.

1759
The British Museum opens to the public in London.

1760–1820
Reign of George III, grandson of George II.

Great Britain

After unifying with Scotland in the early 18th century, the Stuart monarchs of England were succeeded by the Hanoverian kings of Great Britain. Three Georges ruled the country from 1714 to the end of the century. This was a period of great economic change, as the Industrial Revolution gathered pace. By mid-century Britain controlled the world's greatest empire, but it sustained a serious loss when its North American colonies broke away in 1783. Ten years later, Britain was again at war with France.

Parliamentary System
The first Hanoverian king, George I, knew little of British politics and did not speak English well. He relied on his council of ministers, and his chief minister Robert Walpole (1676–1745) took control of the council. This was the beginning of the British cabinet system of government. Walpole (*left*) became first lord of the treasury for the second time in 1721, chairing cabinet meetings. He was effectively prime minister (Britain's first), though the title was not used at the time.

GREAT BRITAIN

NORTH SEA
SCOTLAND
IRELAND
ENGLAND

Jacobite Invasion / Rebellions
In 1715 and 1745 there were two rebellions in support of James Edward Stuart, son of James II (Stuart king 1685–88). The Catholic supporters of the Stuarts were called Jacobites, from Jacobus, *the Latin form of James. The Highland Scots supporting the second rebellion won a victory at Prestonpans in 1745, but were heavily defeated the following year. The map shows Hanoverian unified Britain, with the route taken by Jacobite forces in the second rebellion.*

Territory united under the Crown, 1603
Territory united under the Act of Union, 1707
→ Route of Jacobite forces, 1745–46

Below: Georgian London was busy, noisy, and full of crime. One of the biggest problems was an enormous consumption of alcohol, especially gin, among the city's poor.

Enlightenment Ideas
English philosopher John Locke was a believer in empiricism, the theory that all human knowledge comes from sense impressions. Locke had great faith in experimental science and confidence in the basic goodness of humanity. Along with the French philosophers, he was a pioneer of Enlightenment ideas. He wrote two treatises on government, which influenced many people's ideas of liberal democracy and civil rights.

John Locke (1632–1704) was born in the west of England and studied at Oxford University.

London

Eighteenth-century London was the hub of Great Britain. During the century its area more than doubled, and by 1800 it had a million inhabitants and was the largest city in the world. Wealthy Londoners had fashionable houses built around well-designed squares, but the city's poor lived in squalid conditions. Many came to the capital to look for work, but they ended up on the streets or in workhouses.

A bird's-eye view of Grosvenor Square, in London's fashionable Mayfair district, about 1754. The square had been designed about 30 years earlier as the centerpiece of a great family estate.

The Elite

All European states recognized a noble elite, who were thought to set the standard for society and whose privileges were established by governments and protected by law. The sense of rank became more rigid throughout the century, and the greatest characteristic and aim of the aristocracy was the ownership of land. Wealth was passed on and inherited rather than earned. In France, a nobleman could even lose rank if he worked.

Noblemen had the time and education to interest themselves in architecture, music, and literature. Aristocratic ladies spent a great deal of time on elegant, fashionable dress and the art of polite conversation.

Eighteenth-Century Society

The most striking feature of 18th-century society was the very distinct contrast between the upper, middle, and lower classes. People of different social standing had entirely different experiences of life. The greatest changes came about through the rise of the bourgeoisie. As the middle class grew wealthier, the plight of the laboring poor—especially in the growing towns—became even worse. The class divide widened, leading to revolutionary conflict before the end of the century.

This decorative silver gilt chocolatière (drinking-chocolate pot) and warmer were made in Paris around 1730. Chocolate, coffee and cocoa were popular with the rich.

Peasants

Peasants made up the majority of the 18th-century European population. Many were still totally dependent on agriculture, but during the century there was a great move to the growing towns, turning rural peasants into urban laborers. In Western Europe most peasants were free, whereas in the East many were serfs who could be bought and sold.

This typical English scene shows the marked contrast between elite landowners and those who worked for them. Noble houses required a great deal of upkeep. Workers and servants toiled for long hours behind the scenes of high society.

The Middle Class

The bourgeoisie (originally the inhabitants of walled towns) formed the middle class of the social hierarchy, between the aristocracy and peasantry. They were made up of merchants, traders, businessmen, and other townspeople. During the Industrial Revolution they took on the role of managing machine-minders and other workers. The bourgeoisie supported the rights of trade and property, as well as personal and civil liberty.

Design for a wealthy merchant's London town house of 1774.

The Coffee House

Coffee houses were centers of business and culture. Middle-class merchants, politicians, and writers used them as their club, visiting at regular hours so that their friends and colleagues knew where to find them. In 1730 London had about 500 coffee houses, where people went to learn the latest news and discuss political and social events.

These men in a Viennese coffee house are reading and discussing the news.

These Venetian ladies' shoes of the 1760s were made of silk interwoven with gold and silver thread.

Fashion

In high society ladies' fashion was very much led by Paris and the French court of the *ancien regime* (see page 10). In those circles costume was sumptuous and was seen to be of great importance. The expensive silks of the court were copied in linen by dressmakers of slightly lower circles. Elegant embroidery added to the ornamentation of the age.

THE SCIENTIFIC REVOLUTION

1703
Isaac Newton becomes president of the Royal Society of London for the Promotion of Natural Knowledge; two years later he is knighted by Queen Anne.

1720
Edmond Halley (1656–1742) becomes English Astronomer Royal.

1753
Swedish naturalist Carolus Linnaeus (1707–78) classifies plants in his famous Species Plantarum.

1765
First meeting in Birmingham, England, of the Lunar Society, a group of scientists and intellectuals.

1771–78
Carl Scheele of Sweden and Joseph Priestley of England independently discover oxygen.

1781
German-born British astronomer William Herschel (1738–1822) discovers the planet Uranus (which he names the Georgian Star after his patron, King George III).

1785–88
French mathematician and astronomer Pierre-Simon Laplace (1749–1827) publishes five papers demonstrating the stability of the solar system.

1790
The French Academy of Sciences starts work on new universal units of measurement–the metric system.

In 1783 the Montgolfier brothers of France sent two men up in a hot-air balloon. They flew over Paris for 25 minutes.

Studying the Heavens

Many of the astronomical advances of the period were based on an understanding of the law of gravitation. Scientists such as the French mathematician Alexis-Claude Clairaut (1713–65) made great advances in celestial mechanics, especially the motion of the planets and the Moon. By the end of the century astronomers understood that the Sun and planets formed a stable system held together by gravity.

The Scientific Revolution

During the 18th century great advances were made in science, continuing the Scientific Revolution that had begun two centuries earlier. This had its beginnings in astronomy, and following the discoveries of Newton, much knowledge was gained in this period about the motions and especially gravitation of the solar system. An understanding of science was considered essential for any educated person in the Age of Reason. Many enlightened thinkers believed that a similar, methodical approach should be made to social and political issues.

Sir Isaac Newton

The English mathematician, physicist, and astronomer Isaac Newton is known as one of the greatest scientists of all time. His three great discoveries were the law of gravitation, mathematical calculus (invented independently by Gottfried Leibniz) and, in optics, the discovery that light is made up of a spectrum of colors. His great work *Optics* was published in 1704.

PHILOSOPHIÆ
NATURALIS
PRINCIPIA
MATHEMATICA

Left: Isaac Newton (1642–1727) and his great work, Mathematical Principles of Natural Philosophy.

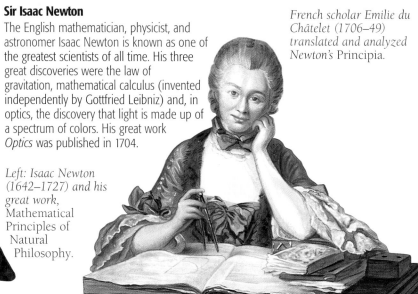

French scholar Emilie du Châtelet (1706–49) translated and analyzed Newton's Principia.

Below: Lavoisier and his wife, from a painting of 1788.

Chemistry

The French chemist Antoine Laurent Lavoisier (1743–94) is known as the founder of modern chemistry. He used his wealth to build a large laboratory, where he discovered in 1778 that air consists of a mixture of two gases, which he called oxygen and nitrogen. He went on to study the role of oxygen in combustion, and published his findings in *Elementary Treatise on Chemistry* (1789), which is regarded as the first chemistry textbook.

Below: Painting of A Philosopher Lecturing on the Orrery by Joseph Wright (1734–97). An orrery was a model of the solar system, often driven by clockwork, which showed the motions of the planets.

Mathematics

The most famous work of the celebrated French mathematician Joseph-Louis Lagrange was *Analytical Mechanics* (1788). Lagrange used algebra to study forces, motions such as planetary orbits, the flow of liquids, and the vibration of strings. Frederick the Great invited "the greatest mathematician in Europe" to his court. Later, Louis XVI gave him apartments in the Louvre. Unlike Lavoisier, Lagrange survived the French Revolution and went on to head the commission that produced the metric system of units.

Below: Portrait of Joseph-Louis Lagrange (1736–1813).

Eighteenth-Century Arts and Architecture

ARTS AND ARCHITECTURE

1710
Sir Christopher Wren (1632–1723) completes St. Paul's Cathedral in London.

1712
Antoine Watteau (1684–1721) is accepted at the French Royal Academy of Painting and Sculpture.

1728
Parisian painter of still lifes and domestic scenes Jean-Baptiste-Siméon Chardin (1699–1779) is a member of the Royal Academy.

1762–64
Venetian Rococo painter Giovanni Battista Tiepolo (1696–1770) decorates the Royal Palace in Madrid.

1762–71
French Rococo sculptor Claude Michel Clodion (1738–1814) works in Rome.

1765
Painter and designer François Boucher (1703–70) becomes director of the French Royal Academy.

1768
Foundation of the Royal Academy of Arts in London, by George III with Sir Joshua Reynolds (1723–92) as its first president.

Early in the century the Baroque style of art and architecture evolved into Rococo, though the word itself was introduced only toward the end of the period. Many art historians see Rococo as a reaction against the excessive, ceremonial splendor of Louis XIV's Versailles. The new gentler, more graceful style spread through Europe from France, influencing all art forms. It was particularly important in central Europe, where it continued after France had started to turn toward a sterner Neoclassical style.

This French Rococo clock of around 1780 is decorated with flowers and Meissen porcelain figures.

Embarkation for the Island of Cythera, a famous Rococo oil painting of 1717 by Antoine Watteau, took travel to the Temple of Love as its subject.

Rococo Style

Rococo (from the French for a rock or shell design) found its fullest expression around 1730 in France. This elegant style of interior decoration was full of curved forms and asymmetrical arrangements, giving a delicate effect of intimacy. Rococo painters developed this into the *fête galante* ("elegant festival"), which showed gatherings of elegantly dressed figures in gardens and parks.

This lacquered commode decorated with flowers and garlands is typical of the 18th-century Venetian school of cabinetmakers.

The Queen's Painter

Louise-Elisabeth Vigée-Lebrun (1755–1842) was one of the most successful of all women painters, and was noted for her portraits of women. In 1779 she was called to Versailles to paint a portrait of Marie Antoinette, and over the years she became a friend of the queen and painted at least 25 portraits of her. Vigée-Lebrun became a member of the male-dominated French Royal Academy in 1783. After the Revolution she traveled and worked in many European cities, including Rome, Vienna, Berlin, St. Petersburg, and London.

Detail from Self Portrait in a Straw Hat by Louise-Elisabeth Vigée-Lebrun.

Rococo Architecture

In architecture, the Rococo style was best expressed in the palaces, churches, and monasteries of southern Germany and Austria, where it merged with the Baroque tradition. The new style was used to transform earlier buildings, such as the 11th-century monastery church at Rottenbuch, in Bavaria. Originally Romanesque, then extended in Gothic style, the church was decorated in Rococo by the architect Joseph Schmuzer in the 1740s.

Schmuzer's stuccoed interior of Rottenbuch church, with frescoes by Matthäus Günther, who became director of the Augsburg Academy in 1762.

St. Paul's Cathedral in London, completed in Sir Christopher Wren in 1710.

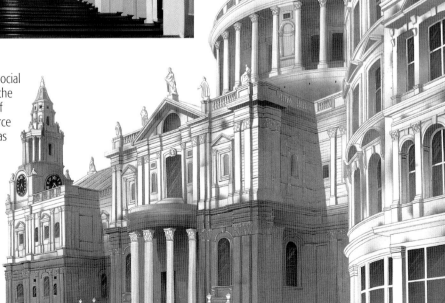

Shipley's Society later gained a royal charter. The RSA building in London was designed by the brothers Robert and James Adam.

Art in England

In 1754 the English painter and social activist William Shipley founded the Society for the Encouragement of Arts, Manufactures, and Commerce in London. One of its aims was to "refine art," and Gainsborough and Reynolds were two early members (before they founded the Royal Academy of Arts). The Society offered prizes, while the Royal Academy conducted art schools. Early students at the art school included J.M.W. Turner in 1789 and John Constable 10 years later.

The closer combination of music and drama made opera popular with 18th-century audiences. Mozart was an expert at developing characterization in his operatic works.

Handel and Bach

Baroque music reached its greatest heights in the work of these two composers. Much of Bach's work is religious, including cantatas and organ compositions for church services. He combined melodies and harmonies, but was better known in his lifetime as an organist than as a composer. Handel's style combines the vigor of the late German Baroque with English and Italian qualities of clarity and charm.

Portrait of J.S. Bach, who wrote masterful works in almost every musical form known at the time.

Eighteenth-Century Music

The first half of the century saw the climax of the Baroque period in music, which featured elaborate, expressive forms. Chamber and orchestra music flourished, and vocal forms such as the oratorio and cantata were introduced. The Classical period began around 1750, at a time when public concerts became more popular with the growing middle class. Composers began introducing more contrast between the different movements of a work, increasing the expression of emotions.

The Opera and the Ballet

Classical opera was greatly influenced by the German composer Christoph Gluck (1714–87), who brought operatic drama and music closer together. Mozart was the greatest exponent of the art. By mid-century ballet was also combining music and dance with the story of a composition. This developing technique was discussed in 1760 by the French choreographer Jean-Georges Noverre in his famous Letters on Dancing and Ballet.

Detail of a painting of the great ballerina Marie Camargo (1710–70), who danced for the Paris Opéra company.

Vivaldi

Antonio Vivaldi was the greatest master of Italian Baroque, and particularly violin music. Ordained a priest in 1703, Vivaldi spent much of his life in Venice. He taught violin at a music conservatory for orphaned girls, and in 1725 composed his most famous works, the violin concertos known as *The Four Seasons*. He wrote concertos for almost every instrument known at the time in Europe.

Portrait of Vivaldi, who helped standardize the 3-movement form of the concerto.

Mozart

Mozart showed amazing musical talent at a very young age, playing for the Austrian empress at the age of 6. Born in Salzburg, Mozart settled in Vienna as a composer, musician, and teacher. He wrote in almost every musical form, combining a beauty of sound with grace and technical perfection. Poverty and overwork led to his death at the age of 35, possibly from typhus.

The young Mozart performing with his father Leopold, who took him on a musical tour of Europe, and older sister Maria Anna.

Beethoven

Born in Bonn, Beethoven studied in Vienna with Haydn and settled there in 1792. At the age of 30 he started to go deaf, but this not stop him composing. His early masterpieces were influenced by Haydn and Mozart, and his revolutionary compositions crowned the Classical period and led into the following, Romantic era in music.

Left: Portrait of Beethoven, who is recognized as one of the world's greatest composers.

End of the Monarchy

Two months after the approval by the new National Assembly of the Declaration of the Rights of Man and of the Citizen, King Louis XVI and his family were taken forcibly from Versailles. They were made to live under guard in the Tuileries Palace in Paris. A new constitution established a limited monarchy, leaving the king with little authority. In 1791 Louis made a failed attempt to escape from the capital, and then formally accepted the constitution. Sixteen months later he was executed.

Marie Antoinette (1755–93), Louis XVI's wife, encouraged him to oppose revolutionary changes.

The French Revolution

Class conflict and a need for social reform in 18th-century France (see pages 10–11) led to rebellion by the people. The political upheavals that took place between 1789 and 1799 are known as the French Revolution. During this period the monarchy was overthrown and different forms of republican administration were successively introduced. After a brutal Reign of Terror, a Directory government led the republic for the rest of the period.

Storming of the Bastille

The Bastille fortress, where political prisoners were held, was seen by the people as a symbol of the monarchy. On July 14, 1789, a large crowd of Parisians stormed the prison, where they hoped to find weapons to fight the king's army. At the same time there were massive peasant uprisings against nobles and their country estates. The revolution was underway.

The revolutionary crowd overpowered soldiers guarding the Bastille and killed the prison governor. They released the prisoners, who numbered just seven.

The Guillotine

The physician Joseph-Ignace Guillotin was elected to the National Assembly in 1789. Believing that executions should be quick and painless, he had a law passed that introduced a beheading machine. This came to be known as the guillotine. The victim was placed face down on the bench, and the heavy blade fell between the uprights to cut off his or her head.

The guillotine, which was first used in April, 1792. It replaced the axe used for beheading nobles and the rope for hanging common criminals.

Volunteers from Marseille marched to an army song that became known as the Marseillaise. It was adopted as the national anthem in 1795.

The Reign of Terror

In 1793 a radical political group called the Jacobins gained control of the National Convention. Led by Maximilien Robespierre, they put a Committee of Public Safety in charge of the republic. From June 1973 to July 1974 the Committee acted brutally against anyone who dared go against official policies of the republic. Thousands of suspects were arrested, and many were guillotined.

Portrait of Maximilien Robespierre (1758–94), who made many enemies and was himself executed by order of the Convention.

A Parisian fighter in the long trousers that caused republicans to be called sans-culottes ("without knee breeches").

The Republic

The new National Assembly reorganized France's old provinces into 83 departments. They were run by elected councils, but the right to vote was limited to male citizens who paid more than a certain level of taxes. The Assembly seized church lands, which were sold to pay off some of the republic's huge debt, and closed monasteries. The newly elected Legislative Assembly made way for a National Convention that declared France a republic in September 1792.

MARCHE DES MARSEILLOIS

Sans culotte Parisien.

Ink well in the shape of a revolutionary red woolen hat crushing a clergyman.

Revolutionary Wars

The French Revolutionary Wars, fought over a decade from 1792 until 1802, began in an effort to defend the revolution. The conflicts took place between France and several European states, growing into wars of French conquest under the leadership of Napoleon. They are usually divided into wars against a First and Second Coalition of allied countries, during which time France was continuously at war with Britain. Following the uneasy peace of the Treat of Amiens in 1802, the Napoleonic Wars went on for another 13 years.

Coalition Against France

In 1793 Britain, the United Provinces (Netherlands), Sardinia, and Spain joined Austria and Prussia in a First Coalition against France. By 1797 all France's opponents had agreed peace treaties, apart from Britain. In a Second Coalition (1798–1802) Britain was joined by the Ottoman Empire, Naples, Russia, Portugal, and Austria. After victories by Napoleon, Britain at last made peace with France in 1802.

An Austrian soldier in 1798.

Rise of Napoleon

In 1795 the French general, Napoleon Bonaparte, put down a rebellion against the revolutionary National Convention. The following year Napoleon was appointed to command the French army in Italy. In 1799 he overthrew the Directory government and assumed dictatorial power as First Consul. As the people's hero, Napoleon was elected Emperor of France in 1804.

Detail from a painting showing Napoleon (1769–1821) as a young military commander.

This 30-soldi coin of the Cisalpine Republic is dated Year IX in the French Republican Calendar (September 1800–01).

New Republics

After winning great victories, the French revolutionary forces gained the Dutch Republic in 1795 and renamed it the Batavian Republic (see page 30). The following year, Napoleon took command of the poorly equipped French forces in northern Italy. After several victories over the Austrians, Napoleon formed the Cisalpine Republic, with Milan as its capital. French victories also created a new Roman Republic, Parthenopean Republic (Naples), and Helvetic Republic (Switzerland).

7 Battle of the Nile

In 1798 Napoleon invaded Egypt in an attempt to destroy British trade with the Middle East and control of India. The French naval forces defeated the Egyptian Mamelukes near Cairo. But just 11 days later, the French fleet of 13 ships of the line and 4 frigates under Admiral Brueys was destroyed in Aboukir Bay by a British fleet commanded by Admiral Horatio Nelson. The victory left the French stranded in Egypt and gave Britain control of the Mediterranean.

FRENCH REPUBLIC AND DEPENDENCIES 1797

KINGDOM OF GREAT BRITAIN

RUSSIAN EMPIRE

KINGDOM OF PRUSSIA

FRENCH REPUBLIC AND DEPENDENCIES

KINGDOM OF AUSTRIA

KINGDOM OF SPAIN

MEDITERRANEAN SEA

French Republic and dependencies

Prussia

Austria

Boundaries of Holy Roman Empire

The Treaties

A peace settlement was signed by France and Austria in 1797 at a village near Udine. It marked the end of Napoleon's successful campaign against the First Coalition. The treaty enlarged French territory, giving the Republic possessions in the Low Countries, on the left bank of the Rhine, and in Lombardy and Mantua. The map shows the dependencies of the French Republic in 1797 following the treaty.

REVOLUTIONARY WARS

1791
Declaration of Pillnitz, in which Austria and Prussia call for reestablishment of the French king.

1792
France declares war on Austria.

1794
French forces win the Battle of Fleurus (in modern Belgium) against the Austrians and Dutch.

1796
Napoleon marries Josephine de Beauharnais.

1797–1802
Period of the Cisalpine Republic.

1798
Napoleon wins the Battle of the Pyramids against the Mamelukes near Cairo.

1798–1802
Period of the Helvetic Republic.

1799
Napoleon wins the Battle of Aboukir against the Ottoman Turks.

1799–1802
Period of the Parthenopean Republic.

1802
The Treaty of Amiens (signed by France, Britain, Spain, and the Batavian Republic) ends 10 years of war.

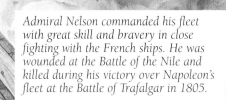

Admiral Nelson commanded his fleet with great skill and bravery in close fighting with the French ships. He was wounded at the Battle of the Nile and killed during his victory over Napoleon's fleet at the Battle of Trafalgar in 1805.

Glossary

Absolute monarchy A form of government where a king or queen has complete, or absolute, control over every aspect of the lives of his or her subjects. Absolute monarchs may claim to be accountable to God alone.

Ambassador Someone who goes abroad to represent the interests of a ruler or government at a foreign court or government.

Architecture The art of designing and then supervising the construction of buildings.

Aristocracy A ruling class of people, usually families or dynasties, who inherit power, land, and wealth.

Authoritarian A form or government where the state is very powerful and individuals have few rights or freedoms.

Autocracy A form of government in which the political power is held by a single, self-appointed ruler, known as an "autocrat."

Censorship When a government controls what may be printed in books or newspapers, and removes information that it does not want to be made public.

Civil war Armed conflict between different groups of people from the same country.

Clergy the official religious leaders of a given religion. Priests, nuns, and bishops are some examples of the clergy in most Christian churches.

Colony A country's overseas land or territory.

Court The place where a monarch or ruler lives, including the buildings as well as all the courtiers (the other people who live there).

Deism The belief that a supreme God exists who created the physical universe, and that religious truths can be arrived at by the application of reason and observation of the natural world.

Despotism A form of rule where all power is in the hands of one person or a small group of people. A despot is someone who rules this way.

Devout To be very religious.

Diplomacy The art of managing international relations with other countries through negotiation rather than by warfare.

Divine right of kings A political and religious system where the king or queen is not controlled by a parliament, aristocracy, or any other group but is believed to rule directly under God.

Dynasty A line of rulers coming from the same family, or a period during which they reign.

Economy The wealth and resources of a country or a region.

Empire All of the land controlled by a ruler or government, including overseas territories.

Empiricism In philosophy, a theory which says that knowledge comes from experience and evidence rather than from innate ideas.

Heir The next in line to the throne, who will become ruler when the current ruler dies or abdicates (abandons the title).

Jacobites Followers of the late-17th century political movement dedicated to the return of the Stuart kings to the thrones of England and Scotland.

Jesuits Members of a Roman Catholic religious order called the Society of Jesus founded by Saint Ignatius of Loyola in 16th century Spain.

Minister An important official who serves a ruler or in a government.

Monarchy A country in which the ruler is a king or queen who rules by right of birth rather than by being elected.

Noble A high-ranking person who is a member of the aristocracy. They may be noble by birth, or be awarded their title.

Obsolete Something that is out of date or old fashioned and has been replaced by something better and more advanced.

Orrery A mechanical device that shows the relative positions and motions of the planets and moons in the solar system.

Parliament A formal gathering of people that debates and decides a country's laws. Members of parliament may be chosen by an election.

Philosophy The study of human thought about the meaning of life and the correct way to live.

Policy The course of action decided by a ruler, minister, government, or parliament.

Uprising An organized attempt to oppose authority; a conflict in which one group tries to take control from another. Similar in meaning to rebellion.

Rebel To rise up and challenge a ruler or government, sometimes by force; also the name for a person who does this.

Reform To change an organization or system to make it work better or more efficiently.

Regent Someone who governs on behalf of a young prince or princess who inherits the throne before they are old enough officially to become the next king or queen.

Republic A country in which the ruler, such as the Stadholder in the Netherlands, is elected and is not a monarch who rules by birthright.

Revolution A change in power or government which occurs in a short period of time, often as a result of violents protests and struggle.

Secular Something that is not religious, for example a government, country, organization, festival, or building.

Serf A farm laborer who works on the land but does not own it. The serf's labor is given in exchange for protection by the landowner and the right to work the land.

Shipwright Someone who builds ships.

Siege The surrounding of a city or fort by the army of their enemy in an attempt to capture it. A siege can last many days with the intention of starving the people inside so that they will surrender.

Subject A person who lives under the rule of a king or queen.

Tax Money people must pay to a government, church, or ruler to help support them or a particular cause.

Treaty A written agreement between two or more countries or rulers, often drawn up at the end of a war.

Index

Abdulhamid I, Ottoman sultan 5, 24
Aboukir Bay 44
Act of Union 32
Adam, James 39
Adam, Robert 39
Adriatic Sea 15
Aegean Sea 24
Age of Reason 5, 6, 8, 36
Ahmed III, Ottoman sultan 4, 24
American War of Independence 30
Amsterdam 5, 30, 31
Ancien Régime 10
Anna I, Empress of Russia 21
Anne, of Hanover, Princess Royal
 and Princess of Orange 30
Aragon 12
Austria/Austrian 4, 5, 7, 12, 13, 14,
 16, 19, 21, 23, 24, 39, 40, 41, 44, 45
Azov 21, 24

Bach, Johann Sebastian 40
Bakhchisarai 25
Balkans 24
Baltic Sea 20
Bank of England 7
Baroque 38, 39, 40
Batavian Republic 5, 30, 44, 45
Bath 38
Batoni, Pompeo 26
Battle of Aboukir 45
Battle of Blenheim 7
Battle of Culloden 32
Battle of Fleurus 45
Battle of the Nile 45
Battle of the Pyramids 45
Battle of Trafalgar 45
Bavaria 7, 39
Beethoven, Ludwig van 40, 41
Belgium 30, 45
Berlin 7, 38
Birmingham 36
Black Sea 22, 24, 25
Bobrinskoy, Alexei 23
Bohemia 16
Bonn 41
Bosnia-Herzegovina 24
Boswell, James 26, 27
Boucher, François 38
Bourbon 12, 13
Bourbon Reforms 12
Brabant 30
Braganza dynasty 12
Brandenburg 18
Britain/British 5, 6, 7, 11, 12, 20, 30,
 31, 44, 45
Brueys, François-Paul Brueys
 d'Aigalliers, Comte de Brueys,
 Admiral 44

Bulgaria 24

Cairo 44
Camargo, Marie 41
Cameron, Charles 23
Canada 11
Canaletto (Canal, Antonio), 15, 38
Caspian Sea 4, 21
Catalonia 12
Catherine I, Empress of Russia 21
Catherine II, "the Great", Empress of
 Russia 5, 9, 22, 23, 24
Chardin, Jean-Baptiste-Siméon 38
Charles II, King of Spain 4, 12
Charles III King of Spain, Naples and
 Sicily, Duke of Parma 5, 12, 13, 15,
 16
Charles VI, Holy Roman Emperor 16
Charles VII, Holy Roman Emperor 14
China 30
Christian VII, King of Denmark and
 Norway 5
Cisalpine Republic 44, 45
Clement XII, Pope 14
Clodion, Claude Michel 9, 38
Comte de Bonneval, Claude
 Alexandre 24
Comtesse du Barry, Marie-Jeannette
 Becù 11
Constable, John 39
Constantinople 22
Corsica 14, 26
Courland, duchy of 22
Crimea 5, 22, 23, 24, 25
Crimean Tartars 25

d'Alembert, Jean 9
de Fleury, André-Hercule, cardinal
 11
Declaration of Pillnitz 45
Declaration of the Rights of Man 5,
 6, 42
Denmark 5
Denmark-Norway 4, 21
Deptford 20
Diderot, Denis 5, 8, 9, 26
Duchy of Parma and Piacenza 15
Duchy of Prussia 18
Duchy of Tuscany 16
du Châtelet, Emilie, marquise 36
Dutch East India Company 5, 30
Dutch Patriots 31
Dutch Republic 12, 30, 44

Egypt 44
Elizabeth I, Empress of Russia 4, 21,
 22, 23
Encyclopédie 5, 8, 26

England / English 4, 12, 13, 31, 32,
 35, 36, 40
Enlightenment 5, 6, 7, 8, 22
Epirus 24
Estonia 20

Falconet, Etienne-Maurice 23
Farnese, Antonio, duke of Parma
 and Piacenza 14
Farnese Family 15
Ferdinand I, King of Naples and
 Sicily 14
Ferdinand VI, King of Spain 4, 12
Florida 12
Fourth Anglo-Dutch War 30
Fragonard, Jean-Honoré 38
France / French 4, 5, 6, 7, 8, 10, 12,
 16, 17, 19, 26, 30, 31, 32, 34, 35, 36,
 38, 40, 42, 43, 44, 45
Francis I, Holy Roman Emperor,
 Grand Duke of Tuscany, Duke of
 Lorraine 15, 16, 17
Francis II, Holy Roman Emperor 16
Frederick II, "the Great," of Prussia
 4, 7, 9, 16, 18, 19, 37
Frederick III, elector of Brandenburg
 18
Frederick William I, King of Prussia
 18
Frederick William II, King of Prussia
 5, 30
French Revolution 5, 37, 42
French Revolutionary Wars 7

Gainsborough, Thomas 38, 39
Galicia 16
Genoa 14, 15
Geoffrin, Marie-Thérèse 9
George I, King of England 18, 32
George II, King of England, 32
George III, King of England, 32, 36,
 38
Germany / German 21, 39, 40
Gibraltar 12
Gluck, Christoph Willibald Ritter von
 41
Godin, Isabella 6
Goethe, Johann Wolfgang von 26
Gothic 39
Goya, Francisco 12, 15
Grand Tour 26
Great Britain 4, 30, 32, 33
Great Northern War 4, 21
Greece 24
Greek Orthodox Christians 24
Guastalla 13
Guillotin, Joseph-Ignace 43
Gunther, Matthaus 39

Habsburg-Lorraine family 15
Habsburgs 4, 12, 14, 15, 16, 19, 30
Hague, The 31
Halley, Sir Edmond 36
Handel, George Frederick 40
Hanover 18
Hanoverian kings 32
Haydn, Franz Joseph 40, 41
Helvetic Republic (Switzerland) 44,
 45
Herculaneum 26
Herschel, William 36
Highland Scots 32
Hogarth, William 32
Hohenzollern Castle 18
Hohenzollerns 18, 19
Holy Roman Empire 16, 17, 18
House of Orange 30
House of Savoy 14
Hungary 16

India 44
Industrial Revolution 6, 32, 35
Ingria 20
Islam 24
Italian 40
Italy 14, 26
Ivan IV 21

Jacobites 32
James II, King of England 32
Jesuits 12
John V, King of Portugal 13
Johnson, Samuel 26
Joseph 13
Joseph I, Holy Roman Emperor 16
Joseph I, King of Portugal 5, 12
Joseph II, Holy Roman Emperor 5,
 9, 16, 17, 25
Josephine de Beauharnais, Empress
 of France 45
Juvarra, Filippo 14

Kant, Immanuel 18
Kaynardzha 24
Kingdom of Naples and Sicily 13, 14

Lagrange, Joseph-Louis 37
Laplace, Pierre-Simon 36
Lavoisier, Antoine Laurent 37
Leibniz, Gottfried 36
Leopold I, Holy Roman Emperor 18
Leopold II, Holy Roman Emperor,
 King of Hungary and Moravia 5, 15,
 16, 17
Leopold, Prince of Anhalt-Dessau 18
Leopoldovna, Anna, Grand Duchess
 of Russia 21

Leszczynska, Maria, queen consort of France 11
Lessing, Gotthold Ephraim 18
Linnaeus, Carolus (Linné, Carl) 36
Lisbon 13
Lithuanian 21
Livonia 20
Lodomeria 16
Lombardy 45
London 7, 32, 33, 35, 38, 39
Longhi, Pietro 26
Louis de Boulogne 10
Louis XIV, King of France 7, 10, 12, 38
Louis XV, King of France 4, 5, 9, 10, 11
Louis XVI, King of France 5, 7, 10, 11, 37, 42, 43
Louvre 37
Low Countries 30
Lucca 14, 15
Ludovico Manin 14
Luis I, King of Spain 12
Luxembourg 30

Madrid 38
Mahmud I, Ottoman sultan 4, 24
Mamelukes 44, 45
Mantua 45
Maria I, Queen of Portugal 5, 12
Maria Theresa of Austria, Holy Roman Empress, Queen of Hungary and Bohemia 4, 5, 15, 16, 17
Marie Antoinette, Queen consort of France 11, 16, 38, 42, 43
Marseille 43
Medici, Gian Gastone de' 15
Methuen Treaty 12
Middle East 44
Milan 14, 44
Minorca 12
Montesquieu, Baron de 8, 9, 22
Montgolfier brothers 36
Moscow 22
Mozart, Maria Anna 41
Mozart, Wolfgang Amadeus 5, 40, 41
Mustafa III, Ottoman sultan 24

Naples 4, 44
Napoleon I, of France, Bonaparte 7, 44, 45
Napoleonic Wars 44
Nassau 31
Nelson, Horatio, Admiral 44, 45
Neoclassical 38
Netherlands 4, 30
Newton, Sir Isaac 6, 36
North American colonies 32
North American empire 5

Northern War 24
Noverre, Jean-Georges 41
Norway 5
Nugent, Thomas 26

Orangists 31
Ottoman Empire 24, 44
Ottoman Turks 22, 24, 25, 45

Pannini, Giovanni Paolo 27
Paoli, Pasquale 26
Papal States 14, 15
Paris 5, 6, 9, 26, 34, 35, 36, 42
Parma 13, 14
Parthenopean Republic (Naples) 44, 45
Patriot Revolution 30
Paul I, Emperor of Russia 5, 23
Persia 4, 21
Peter I, of Russia, "the Great" 4, 20, 21, 22, 23, 24
Peter II, Emperor of Russia 21
Peter III, King of Portugal 5
Peter III 12, 22, 23
Peter Leopold, Grand Duke of Tuscany 5, 14
Petrovna, Anna, Grand Duchess of Russia 23
Philip V, King of Spain 4, 12
Philippe Charles of Orléans, Duke of Orléans 11
Philosophes 9
Piacenza 13, 14
Piedmont 14
Piedmont-Sardinia 14
Poland 5, 11, 16, 18, 19, 22, 23
Pombal, Marquess de 5, 13
Pomerania 18
Pomerelia 19
Pompadour, Jeanne de 5, 9, 11
Pompeii 26
Portugal 12, 13, 44
Potemkin, Grigory 23
Potsdam 18
Prestonpans 32
Priestley, Joseph 36
Pronk, Cornelis 30
Prussia/Prussians 5, 7, 11, 16, 17, 18, 19, 21, 23, 31, 44, 45

Queen Anne, Queen of Great Britain 32, 36

Rameau, Jean-Philippe 40
Rastrelli, Bartolomeo 21
Reign of Terror 5, 42, 43
Revolutionary Wars 44, 45
Reynolds, Sir Joshua 38, 39
River Dniester 25
River Pruth 24
River Rhine 45

Robespierre, Maximilien 43
Rococo 38, 39
Romanesque 39
Romantic era 41
Rome 14, 26, 27, 38
Rottenbuch 39
Rousseau, Jean-Jacques 8, 9, 26
Russia/Russians 4, 5, 7, 16, 19, 20, 21, 22, 23, 24, 25, 44
Russian Orthodox Church 21, 22
Russo-Turkish War 24

Salvi, Nicolo 14
Salzburg 41
Sarajevo 5, 24
Sardinia 4, 14, 44
Saxony-Poland 4, 21
Scheele, Carl Wilhelm 36
Schmuzer, Joseph 39
Scientific Revolution 36
Scotland 32
Second Russo-Turkish War 24
Second Turkish War 25
Selim III, Ottoman sultan 24, 25
Seven Years' War 5, 7, 10, 11, 16, 19, 21, 32
Shipley, William 39
Sicily 4, 14
Silesia 5, 16, 18, 19
Sophie, Princess of Anhalt-Zerbst 22
Spain / Spanish 11, 12, 13, 14, 44, 45
Starov, Ivan 23
St Petersburg 20, 23, 38
Storming of the Bastille 5, 42
Stuart, Charles Edward 32
Stuart, James Edward 32
Swabia 18
Sweden 4, 21, 36

Talbot, John 26
Tanucci, Bernardo 14
Tiepolo, Giovanni Battista 38
Tischbein, Johann Heinrich Wilhelm 31
Treaty of Aix-la-Chapelle 13, 16
Treaty of Amiens 44, 45
Treaty of Belgrade 24
Treaty of Jassy 25
Treaty of Kuchuk Kainarji 24
Treaty of Stockholm 18
Treaty of Utrecht 14
Tsarskoe Selo 21, 23
Turin 14
Turkey 24
Turkish War 21
Turks 5, 23
Turnhout 30
Turner, J.M.W. 39
Tuscany 5, 14, 15

Udine 45
Uffizi Gallery 27
United Provinces (Netherlands) 30, 44
United States of America 30

Valencia 12
Valenti Gonzaga, Silvio, cardinal 27
Van der Capellen, Joan tot den Pol 30
Venice/Venetian 5, 14, 15, 26, 35, 38, 41
Versailles 26, 38, 42
Victor Amadues II of Savoy 4, 14
Vienna/Viennese 17, 35, 38, 41
Vigée-Lebrun, Louise-Elisabeth 38
Vivaldi, Antonio 40, 41
Voltaire 8, 19, 22, 23
von Kaunitz, Count Wenzel Anton 16

Wales 4, 32
Walpole, Sir Robert 4, 32
War of the Austrian Succession 7, 11, 13, 16
War of the Bavarian Succession 7
War of the Polish Succession 4, 7, 11, 13, 14
War of the Spanish Succession 7, 12, 14, 16
Warsaw 22
Watteau, Jean-Antoine 38
West Prussia 19
Wilhelmina of Prussia 30, 31
William III, Prince of Orange 4, 30
William IV, Prince of Orange and Nassau 4, 30, 31
William V, Prince of Orange and Nassau 30, 31
Wootton, John 7
Wren, Sir Christopher 38, 39
Wright, Joseph 37

Yemelyan Pugachov 22

Zaandam 20
Zoffany, Johann 27